T0298918

Working Collaboratively

A Practical Guide to Achieving More

Penny Walker

www.penny-walker.co.uk

First published in 2013 by Dō Sustainability
87 Lonsdale Road, Oxford OX2 7ET, UK

ISBN 978-1-909293-61-8 (eBook-ePub)
ISBN 978-1-909293-62-5 (eBook-PDF)
ISBN 978-1-909293-60-1 (Paperback)

A catalogue record for this title is available from the British Library.

Dō Sustainability strives for net positive social and environmental impact. See our sustainability policy at **www.dosustainability.com**.

Page design and typesetting by Alison Rayner
Cover by Becky Chilcott

For further information on Dō Sustainability, visit our website:
www.dosustainability.com

DōShorts

Dō Sustainability is the publisher of **DōShorts**: short, high-value ebooks that distil sustainability best practice and business insights for busy, results-driven professionals. Each DōShort can be read in 90 minutes.

New and forthcoming DōShorts – stay up to date

We publish 3 to 5 new DōShorts each month. The best way to keep up to date? Sign up to our short, monthly newsletter. Go to **www.dosustainability. com/newsletter** to sign up to the Dō Newsletter. Some of our latest and forthcoming titles include:

- *Making the Most of Standards*   Adrian Henriques
- *How to Account for Sustainability: A Business Guide to Measuring and Managing*   Laura Musikanski
- *Sustainability in the Public Sector: An Essential Briefing for Stakeholders*   Sonja Powell
- *Sustainability Reporting for SMEs: Competitive Advantage Through Transparency*   Elaine Cohen
- *REDD+ and Business Sustainability: A Guide to Reversing Deforestation for Forward Thinking Companies*   Brian McFarland
- *How Gamification Can Help Your Business Engage in Sustainability*   Paula Owen
- *Sustainable Energy Options for Business*   Philip Wolfe
- *Adapting to Climate Change: 2.0 Enterprise Risk Management* Mark Trexler & Laura Kosloff
- *How to Engage Youth to Drive Corporate Responsbility: Roles and Interventions*   Nicolò Wojewoda

- *The Short Guide to Sustainable Investing* Cary Krosinsky
- *Strategic Sustainability: Why it Matters to Your Business and How to Make it Happen* Alexandra McKay
- *Sustainability Decoded: How to Unlock Profit Through the Value Chain* Laura Musikanski

Subscriptions

In addition to individual sales of our ebooks, we now offer subscriptions. Access 60+ ebooks for the price of 5 with a personal subscription to our full e-library. Institutional subscriptions are also available for your staff or students. Visit **www.dosustainability.com/books/subscriptions** or email **veruschka@dosustainability.com**

Write for us, or suggest a DōShort

Please visit **www.dosustainability.com** for our full publishing programme. If you don't find what you need, write for us! Or suggest a DōShort on our website. We look forward to hearing from you.

....

Abstract

SOME OF OUR BIGGEST CHALLENGES cannot be solved by one organisation or even one sector acting alone. They demand simultaneous, coordinated action by players with different interests and skills. We need to work collaboratively to sort them. And we can!

In this DōShort, Penny Walker takes you through the early steps you need to take to identify likely collaborators, find the common ground and work out how you'll work together.

You'll also hear the inside story from international multi-sector collaborations like the Sustainable Shipping Initiative as well as examples of local cooperation to protect water sources and businesses working together to promote leadership on climate change.

Practical tools include:

- Stakeholder analysis
- Collaborative advantage
- Honest brokers and organic leaders
- Techniques for finding shared outcomes and gauging how much support there is for them

There are case studies, frameworks, insights and tips from people who have built successful collaborations, all packed into a 90 minute read.

"Jump in and see where it takes you!"

About the Author

 **PENNY WALKER** is an independent consultant and has been helping people work towards a more sustainable society for over twenty years, collaborating with people to help them both learn about change and sustainability, and to support them in making a difference.

This work has included projects with Unilever, Greenpeace, the Environment Agency and DECC. She also worked at Friends of the Earth for eight years. She is a Senior Associate of the Cambridge Programme for Sustainability Leadership and an Affiliate of Forum for the Future. She is a director of InterAct Networks, building public sector capacity for stakeholder engagement and collaboration.

Her widely-praised and accessible book, *Change Management for Sustainable Development – a workbook*, was published in 2006. She blogs at **penny-walker.co.uk/blog**

Penny also chairs the award-winning social enterprise Growing Communities (**www.growingcommunities.org**), a literally ground-breaking social enterprise growing and trading food. She lives in North London with her husband, two children and a vegetable garden.

....

Acknowledgments

THIS BOOK HAS DRAWN ON HELP, ideas, experiences and opportunities offered by an appropriately large number of people: Andrew Acland, Cath Beaver, Craig Bennett, Fiona Bowles, Cath Brooks, Signe Bruun Jensen, Ken Caplan, Niamh Carey, Lindsey Colbourne, Stephanie Draper, Lindsay Evans, James Farrell, Chris Grieve, Michael Guthrie, Charlotte Millar, Paula Orr, Helena Poldervaart, Chris Pomfret, Jonathon Porritt, Keith Richards, Clare Twigger-Ross, Neil Verlander, Lynn Wetenhall; others at the Environment Agency; people who have been involved in the piloting of the Catchment Based Approach in England in particular in the Lower Lee, Tidal Thames and Brent; and others who joined in with an InterAct Networks peer learning day on collaboration; and the anonymous reviewers who gave their feedback with no chance of acknowledgement. Thanks to all of you for your help. Any mistakes, of course, remain mine.

Contents

Collaborate – to work jointly on an activity or project

from Latin *col-* 'together' + *laborare* 'to work'

OXFORD ENGLISH DICTIONARY

CHAPTER 1

Start At The End – 'What'

WHAT DO YOU WANT TO ACHIEVE?

A cure for cancer?

World peace?

Let's zoom in a bit to something more realistic. What about:

- Keeping the rise in global average temperature to below 2 degrees C?

- Halving the proportion of people whose income is less than $1.25 a day?

- All water bodies in a particular catchment having a healthy natural species range and abundance of plants, invertebrates and fish?

- A circular economy?

- Protecting and maintaining the ecosystems services provided in a particular area?

These are all classic 'wicked problems': complex, systemic, with lots of uncertainty and no clear solutions that do not also have downsides for some people (Rittel and Webber, 1973). Problems like maintaining ecosystem services or limiting global temperature rises, embody the Tragedy of the Commons (Hardin, 1968): a common resource will be exploited, perfectly rationally, by each individual who has access to it, until it crashes. Sustainable use of a common resource will only come with active management of access to that resource. (Another solution is to privatise it: pretty hard with the atmosphere.)

GoodCo Fish Ltd can decide, altruistically, to stop catching North Atlantic cod because stocks are dangerously low. But if NastyNets Inc. continue to exploit the fishery, GoodCo Ltd's self-regulation is merely symbolic: noble but ineffective at protecting the endangered cod.

The landlord of a building could invest in making it more energy efficient, but if the tenant pays the energy bills directly then the landlord has no incentive to do so. If the bills are rolled up in the rent, the tenant has no incentive to use energy more efficiently. The Sustainable Shipping Initiative recognises this problem of split incentives: 'charterers of energy upgraded vessels stand to save on fuel bunker costs but if owners are not confident that charterers will share these savings, they are unlikely to make the capital investment up front' (Sustainable Shipping Initiative, 2012).

If the outcome you want to achieve requires change at the level of the system, if there's a resource held in common, or if there are split incentives, then what's needed are collective, collaborative approaches where many players act simultaneously.

They can't be solved by one person or organisation acting alone. The positive outcomes can only be achieved by working with others. Collaboration is the key to unlocking our potential as the generation which takes these problems out of the 'too difficult' box and works out how to solve them, together.

Not everything you want to achieve requires collaboration. That's a good thing, because collaboration is hard! It is slow, inherently uncertain and it means sharing control. And it depends on there being willing collaborators who want the same outcome that you do (or, at least, complementary outcomes). So like a fellowship of mismatched heroes setting out on a perilous quest, you should only do it if the prize is worth the pain.

Collaborative advantage

The cost-benefit judgement depends on understanding the potential *collaborative advantage*: the extra you can (only) achieve by working with others, rather than working alone (Huxham, 1993). Huxham waxes rather lyrical:

> *Collaborative advantage will be achieved when something unusually creative is produced – perhaps an objective is met – that no organization could have produced on its own and when each organization, through the collaboration, is able to achieve its own objectives better than it could alone.*

But it's even better than that! Huxham goes on:

> *In some cases, it should also be possible to achieve some higher-level ... objectives for society as a whole rather than just for the participating organizations.*

So collaborative advantage is that truly sweet spot, when not only do you meet goals of your own that you wouldn't be able to otherwise, you can also make things better for people and the planet. Definitely sustainable development territory.

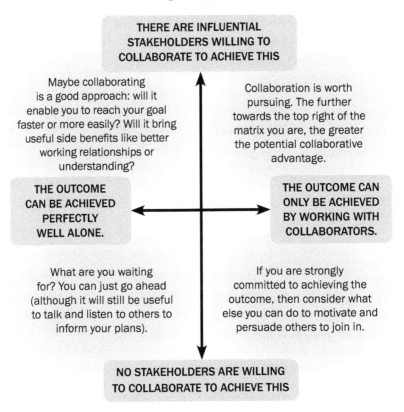

FIGURE 1. Is collaboration a good approach for this outcome?

THERE ARE INFLUENTIAL STAKEHOLDERS WILLING TO COLLABORATE TO ACHIEVE THIS

Maybe collaborating is a good approach: will it enable you to reach your goal faster or more easily? Will it bring useful side benefits like better working relationships or understanding?

Collaboration is worth pursuing. The further towards the top right of the matrix you are, the greater the potential collaborative advantage.

THE OUTCOME CAN BE ACHIEVED PERFECTLY WELL ALONE.

THE OUTCOME CAN ONLY BE ACHIEVED BY WORKING WITH COLLABORATORS.

What are you waiting for? You can just go ahead (although it will still be useful to talk and listen to others to inform your plans).

If you are strongly committed to achieving the outcome, then consider what else you can do to motivate and persuade others to join in.

NO STAKEHOLDERS ARE WILLING TO COLLABORATE TO ACHIEVE THIS

ADAPTED FROM: InterAct Networks and Environment Agency (2013).

Looking at Figure 1, there's another side to the collaborative advantage coin. If the potential collaborative advantage is not high enough, or you can achieve your goals just as well working alone, then it may be that collaboration is not the best approach. You can think of it like this:

The nature of the outcome you are trying to achieve will allow you to map it along the horizontal axis. How wicked, systemic and entrenched is the status quo?

You can make a guess about what other people and organisations want, to do your initial placing along the vertical axis. You may already have had some tentative conversations with people who share your ambition and want to do something, and who realise they'll be more successful acting together. The early exploratory phase (see Figure 1) will help you understand better whether collaboration has potential.

Complementary outcomes

It's likely that other organisations have got an interest in the same issues as you – but they may be looking at it from an entirely different perspective.

The Prince of Wales' Corporate Leaders Group on Climate Change (Corporate Leaders Group) are all from big businesses, so at first sight you might think they all had the same interest, but Craig Bennett, who was Director of the Corporate Leaders Group from 2007 to 2010, explains that they had subtly different needs:

> *I think there were five different sets of motivation, depending on the nature of the business. The heavy emitters knew their businesses would need to change, and wanted some long-term understanding of how that was likely to happen. The technology companies could see an opportunity in low carbon innovation and wanted to accelerate it. Consumer-facing companies were concerned about security in their supply chains as well as public perception and wanted to be seen as leaders. Banks could see that there were*

big-picture economic changes coming, and wanted to be part of shaping the new paradigm. Finally, utilities wanted to get debate and action around adapting to climate change.

....

FIGURE 2. Many outcomes, one project.

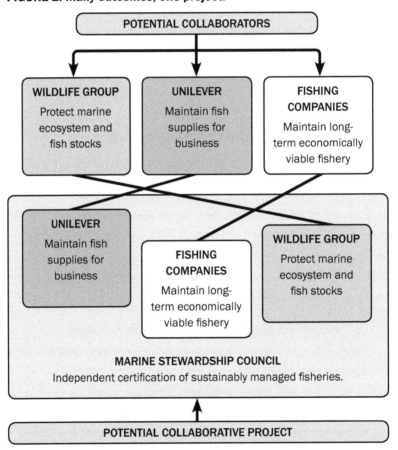

POTENTIAL COLLABORATORS

WILDLIFE GROUP
Protect marine ecosystem and fish stocks

UNILEVER
Maintain fish supplies for business

FISHING COMPANIES
Maintain long-term economically viable fishery

UNILEVER
Maintain fish supplies for business

FISHING COMPANIES
Maintain long-term economically viable fishery

WILDLIFE GROUP
Protect marine ecosystem and fish stocks

MARINE STEWARDSHIP COUNCIL
Independent certification of sustainably managed fisheries.

POTENTIAL COLLABORATIVE PROJECT

ADAPTED FROM: InterAct Networks and Environment Agency (2013).

....

Complementary outcomes were also essential to the success of the Marine Stewardship Council (MSC), see Figure 2. When the MSC was founded Unilever wanted to secure supplies for its international fish business far into the future but could see that there wouldn't be enough fish in the sea for it to meet its business ambitions. WWF wanted to reverse dramatic declines in global fish stocks and protect marine eco-systems threatened by overfishing. A breakthrough came when a small group of fishing and seafood processing companies (the early adopters) began to see that their own interests, of retaining economically viable fisheries now and into the future, could be met only through collaboration in a green-business enterprise offering market-based incentives. Their desired outcomes were complementary, rather than identical. They worked out a way of meeting all three sets of interests simultaneously.

CHAPTER 2

Who Might Collaborate With You?

YOU KNOW THAT WHAT YOU WANT TO ACHIEVE can only be done with others. You've made a first guess that perhaps there are influential potential collaborators out there who might collaborate with you. This is the beginning of the *who* strand.

You also need to:

- Turn that guess into hard facts.

- Begin to understand the complementary skills, constituencies and responsibilities the collaboration needs.

- Assemble a team that can shift the system, which includes the right kinds of leadership.

Bringing together the eventual collaborators can be a long and frustrating phase, when you may not feel as if you are making much progress. Dead-ends, red herrings, people who are supportive in principle but not in practice, having what feels like the same conversation a number of times. This is normal!

Wessex Water's Fiona Bowles had a challenge when approaching stakeholders for their collaboration in the Frome and Piddle Catchment

Pilot. (These pilots experimented with addressing water quality and other problems at a 'catchment' level – that is, a scale bigger than individual rivers or lakes, but smaller than entire river basins.)

Whilst we work regularly with farmers to protect our water supply sources, we found it hard to find farmers or farming organisations who would undertake to represent the views of this interest group on the initial steering group. Once the issues were identified they were more keen to engage.

Guesses into evidence

Don't neglect the obvious desk research: who are the players and commentators, critics and pioneers with an interest in the issues? What have they said about their ambition and about what's holding them back?

But don't do it all by hiding behind your keyboard. Pretty soon, you'll need to have one-to-one conversations with people, to check out your thinking and to understand how they see the system, the future they want to create and the things that need to be tackled collaboratively.

Fiona describes the early search for potential collaborators:

A starting point is to go to or phone each person who may have an interest or a stake, and test the water before taking the big step of offering to host a project. We did a lot of homework – to know the area, who's involved, what the existing plans are. As you work your way through the issues, once the collaboration is underway, you come across additional people. It starts quite small and grows. An organisation will tell you about another one that you hadn't identified earlier.

Collaboration can come about because of chance meetings. The origins of the Corporate Leaders Group can be traced back to the drinks reception after a speech by then Prime Minister Tony Blair in 2004. Senior business leaders were frustrated that the public voice of business seemed to be against government action on climate change, and wanted to get away from the lowest common denominator approach then typified by traditional organisations like the CBI. They chatted informally about how to make sure that the progressive view was heard, and then asked the Cambridge Programme for Sustainability Leadership (then the Cambridge Programme for Industry) to convene a group of ambitious business leaders to put forward an alternative challenge to government.

Complementary collaborators

Effective collaborations are made up of organisations with complementary skills, constituencies and responsibilities. There are lots of reasons for this:

- If the outcome you want to achieve means shifting a system, then you need to have different parts the system acting simultaneously.

- Diversity of perspectives stimulates creativity and innovation.

- Seeing surprising bedfellows committing to work together brings interest and credibility.

- One organisation, however successful, will not have the range of skills needed, nor access to all the relevant parts of the system.

Collaborative approaches to protecting and improving water catchments in the UK typically include the relevant regulator (the Environment Agency), the local water company (e.g. Wessex Water, Anglian Water), a river-specific charity (e.g. the Thames Rivers Trust), local authorities, farming interests and so on. So think widely about the kinds of organisations and people who you need to approach – begin with the ones you are familiar with, by all means, but go beyond them too.

Assemble the team

And how can you begin to assemble a team with a good enough range of super-powers (complementary competencies) to be able to shift the system?

Success in building the team comes from a combination of strategic thinking, common sense and building on your existing networks.

The common sense is to do your homework – who are the obvious first people to contact? Think about what they might want that would make them want to collaborate. Go in with an open mind, but not an empty mind.

What are your existing networks? Begin with who you know, who you can connect with, via networks and organisations.

Pick up the phone and ask people you know, trust, respect and enjoy working with.

Add in some strategic thinking to make sure you don't only approach the usual suspects or the organisations you are comfortable with. If you want to change the system, you need to work with the whole system, not just the bits of it you're already familiar with or think will be natural bedfellows.

This strategic thinking about who to work with is called stakeholder analysis.

Stakeholder analysis

A stakeholder is anyone who can affect, or is impacted by the issue, project, topic or system that you are focusing on.

In the case of potential collaboration, stakeholders will be the people and organisations who play a part in the system, contribute to the problem or its possible solutions, are affected by it, or have an interest in how it might change.

The *first step* is to identify all those people and organisations. Jot down a long-list. Then make it longer. The aim at this stage is to broaden your thinking to go beyond the usual suspects. Use these headings as a checklist:

- *Businesses* – primary suppliers, manufacturers, distributors, retailers, ultimate customers, business groupings or associations.

- *Public bodies* – policy-makers, regulators, service providers.

- *Campaign groups and charities* – environmental, social, ethical or faith-based, amenity, sporting, arts, development, ethnic, community, user groups.

- *Publics* – consumers, residents, demographics, interests.

- *Leaders and focal points* – who must be engaged, for this to have any credibility or leverage?

Other checklists that help ensure you haven't missed anyone are:

- Actors, oilers, blockers (Acland, undated).

- The role different stakeholders might play, for example, legal or regulatory; outreach or lobbying; landowners; those who will earn money from it; those who will be directly affected by it (e.g. employed, living nearby); those who are accountable for it.

Make your list as specific as possible – which team in which government department? Which business unit in which supplier? Which person in which NGO?

Associations, networks or professional bodies may be useful conduits to their members, but be aware of whether, in your particular situation, it is the individual members or the association which is more likely to be the active collaborator. In particular, trade associations, with some noble and notable exceptions, generally operate to the lowest common denominator, because they need to represent the full range of their members' interests: something that the Corporate Leaders Group, for example, sought deliberately to move beyond. Trade associations may be stakeholders who need to be kept informed, but are unlikely to be active collaborators in their own right.

Ask yourself, what headings have been missed off this checklist? Where are my blind spots in relation to this? Who can help me lift the blinkers?

The *second step* is to analyse the list, to help prioritise the organisations or people. This matrix (Figure 3) is very helpful for that analysis.

Step 1: *Identify all the people and organisations.*

Step 2: *Map them on this matrix, according to their degree of influence and the degree of impact on them.*

....

FIGURE 3. Stakeholder analysis matrix A.

	THEY HAVE A HIGH DEGREE OF INFLUENCE ON THE CURRENT SITUATION.	
THE CURRENT SYSTEM OR A CHANGE TO IT WILL HAVE A LOW IMPACT ON THEM.		THE CURRENT SYSTEM OR A CHANGE TO IT WILL HAVE A HIGH IMPACT ON THEM.
	THEY HAVE A LOW DEGREE OF INFLUENCE ON THE CURRENT SITUATION.	

ADAPTED FROM: InterAct Networks and the Environment Agency (2011).

....

Having placed the stakeholders on this map, the *third step* is to see what the implications are.

Step 3: *See what the implications are.*

FIGURE 4. Stakeholder analysis matrix B.

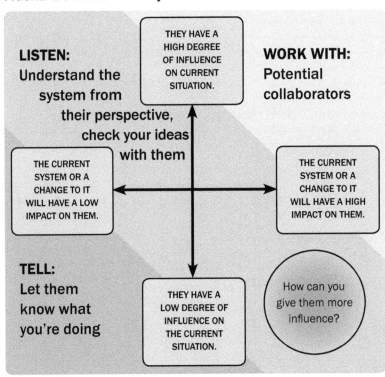

ADAPTED FROM: InterAct Networks and the Environment Agency (2011).

Do your stakeholder analysis with a small team to make use of a diversity of perspectives – ideally, this small team will include some of your warm early enthusiastic collaborators. Flip charts and post-its come in very handy.

Like so much in the early stages of collaboration, there will be some chicken-and-egg going on – you need to identify potential collaborators initially, so you can begin. But then you need to repeat this with the people who first cluster around to work with you, and keep asking yourselves: what is this system, who are the key players, who can have an impact and who will be affected, who can help, who's missing . . .?

Stephanie Draper of Forum for the Future was involved in establishing the Sustainable Shipping Initiative. She says:

> *We did our initial system and stakeholder mapping with a few early players, and approached new key people through that core group and their networks. There was clearly a real appetite for leaders in the industry to work together to break the log-jam, so we gradually found more and more supportive players. We didn't get a perfect match to the stakeholder group that the collaborative group wanted to see (really reflecting the whole supply chain) – some types of organisations just didn't see the mutual interests – but we got good enough (and willing) representation of the system.*

Common but not identical

Collaboration doesn't mean that you need to become like the organisation you are collaborating with, or give up your values or unique mission. Craig Bennett puts it like this:

> *There are two different parties with different strategies, different organisational purpose. The interesting thing is them uniting around common aims, but no-one should pretend that their motives or organisational character is the same. A business doesn't have to become a charity, an NGO doesn't become a business.*

The 'organic leader' and the 'honest broker'

Not an Aesop's fable, but two important kinds of lynchpin figures in successful collaborations. Researchers Chris Ansell and Alison Gash looked at nearly 140 examples of collaborations, and saw that there were two kinds of leadership which were critical to success (Ansell and Gash, 2007). They say:

> *Although 'unassisted' negotiations are sometimes possible, the literature overwhelmingly finds that facilitative leadership is important for bringing stakeholders together and getting them to engage each other in a collaborative spirit.*

What kind of person can provide this facilitative leadership? Do they have to be disinterested, like a classic independent agenda-neutral facilitator? Or do they have to be a figure with credibility and power within the system, to give everyone confidence that change is possible – the sense of agency?

Interestingly, Ansell and Gash think both are needed, depending on the circumstances. The 'honest broker' that everyone can trust – precisely because they don't have an axe to grind – is especially helpful when the collaborators are approximately equally powerful, and all want to get something important to them from the collaboration. This honest broker will pay attention to process and remain above the fray. The 'organic leader' emerges from among the stakeholders and is already respected and trusted by the rest of the stakeholders. Their strength may come from the power and credibility of their organisation as well as personal qualities like technical knowledge, charisma and so on. This role is especially important, say Ansell and Gash:

where power distribution is more asymmetric or incentives to participate are weak or asymmetric.

Time and again, people I spoke to for this book emphasised the role of the facilitator or third party. Craig Bennett advises:

If you have more than a small number of parties, then don't underestimate the value of proper neutral facilitation and a secretariat.

Whether that third party role should be truly neutral was less clear. Signe Bruun Jensen of Maersk Line valued the facilitation combined with the challenge and conscience role that Forum for the Future brought to the Sustainable Shipping Initiative:

You need that challenger role. If you can find it in a facilitator then great – he or she can help create a sense of urgency and purpose that pushes the process along. I think the real challenge is for the facilitator – whether he or she can balance that potential conflict of interest. That's why we ultimately decided to split the role in the later stages of the process.

While you can buy in a neutral facilitator (if you have the resource to do so), you cannot invent a trusted, powerful 'organic' leader if they are not already in the system.

You may be such a person, or you may need to get such a person on board. Jonathon Porritt, Founder Director of Forum for the Future, has been involved in catalysing many collaborative initiatives, including the Sustainable Shipping Initiative. He says:

You have to be able to get the right people into the room at some stage. If you don't have that ability yourself you have to find someone who has.

Doing it again, and again, and again

The chicken-and-egg style iteration you go through in finding collaborators will be familiar as you (collectively) gradually hone in on the shared outcomes you want to achieve, your plans for achieving them and the ways of working or governance you need to agree together. You will need to have some ideas to begin with, and you'll need to make sure the conversations happen, but you'll have the déjà-vu experience of going over the same ground again and again as you build the collaboration and begin to work together, each time more expertly and collaboratively.

. . . .

CHAPTER 3

Co-developing Your Ways of Working – 'How'

HOW WILL YOU WORK TOGETHER?

We were a small group early on, around 16 people talking high-level ideas, so facilitated meetings and consensus was feasible. The later stages were harder. All of a sudden we had a bigger group of people from contrasting corporate cultures having to agree – and get internal sign-off – on very specific projects and commitments. As a result, we had to evolve our way of working together along the way. We are now developing a more formal governance structure with trustees and voting rules. SIGNE BRUUN JENSEN, MAERSK LINE, TALKING ABOUT THE SUSTAINABLE SHIPPING INITIATIVE

Are you a process geek, excited by flow charts, ground rules and post-it notes? If you are, you will love this bit. If not, then let me reassure you that the investment you and your collaborators make early on in agreeing *how* you'll agree, and deciding *how* you'll decide, will be repaid amply when the going gets tough. And there are process-savvy people who can help you – bonus points if they are also honest brokers. If they aren't already in your team, then go out and find them.

First thoughts on how

This strand of work goes hand-in-hand with assembling the team (who) and finding the win-wins (what). And like both of those, it starts low-key and informal. The things to remember are:

- You choose and agree how you work together – there's nothing inevitable about it.

- Share your assumptions and expectations about the how, and your organisation's preferences and needs, so that everyone can see the similarities and differences.

For example, you may expect every meeting to be followed by a short note summarising the decisions which have been taken and the actions which have been agreed. Someone else may assume that these things just get remembered. Your organisation may need you to present a paper to a committee for sign-off before you begin spending serious time on this, which means you will need to wait some weeks or even months between informal soundings and any public commitment to work together. Someone else may have the freedom to develop the work more rapidly.

As long as everyone shares their assumptions, expectations and preferences or needs, then you can collectively choose and agree how to work together in a way that suits you all.

The kinds of questions to consider include:

- Who is 'in' the collaboration? How do we know? How do we decide who to sound out and who to formally invite? What does being 'in' mean (commitments, obligations, etc.)?

- Who is 'leading' the collaboration? (This could be a small working group, or someone in one of the organisations who has been asked to spend some proper time putting it together.) What do we want them to do? What decisions about 'how' we work together can they take alone, and what decisions do we want a wider group of people to be involved with? How much do we want them to check and chase progress?

- Who is resourcing which bits of the process of collaborating? Who is taking on which tasks, to plan, host or run meetings? Who is doing which bits of research and who is pulling it all together? Who is doing the next set of steps to assemble the team? Who is doing the next steps to work up and agree any further points about how to work together? Who is doing the next steps to explore what to work on together?

- Who needs to be involved in making decisions about the next steps in the early phase? Does there need to be a 'holding group' or 'steering group' of some kind? At this stage, how formal or informal does everyone want the meetings to be?

- What are your assumptions about making decisions: will you reach agreement by consensus? By simple majority? Or are you assuming that those on board earliest are the real decision-makers? How will you approach sorting out any differences or disagreements?

As a rule of thumb, you can expect relatively informal ways of working that just emerge without much discussion in the earlier exploratory phase, while the later phases, with larger numbers and weightier decisions to be made, will be more formalised. This formalising means explicitly agreeing the how, and paying attention to whether people are happy with how the collaborators are working together. It doesn't necessarily mean that those ways of working become stiff and all your meetings suddenly have a Chair who has a casting vote – plenty of room for creative, participative workshops and graphic facilitation here too!

If things seem to be stuck or getting fractious, check whether there's a mismatch of people's needs or expectations around process. It isn't the most exciting conversation you will have. Fiona Bowles says:

> *The challenge is that everyone's different backgrounds meant that they had different levels of experience and comfort with 'process'. We did try to lay out a governance model and terms of reference, but people weren't that excited about it. It was signed off easily!*

It was her experience that actually working together on something helped the ways of working to become real.

> *It's the doing things that makes the partnership grow. For us, just having a launch event that we had to organise together made a big difference: an early successful task to get people to work together.*

Conversation starter – principles

Here's a set of principles for collaborative working. For collaboration to be really effective, all of the main collaborators need to be working to these principles, so you can use these as a prompt for conversations about how you work together.

PRINCIPLES FOR COLLABORATIVE WORKING

Focus on outcomes	• Be clear about what outcomes (results in the real world) you all want to achieve. Listen to what each other wants, both in general and from any proposed joint process. • Invest time to reach a shared expression of what you want to achieve that is compelling and clear to all. • Regularly review those outcomes as they may change over time.
Thoroughly explore common ground	• Rather than focusing on the differences, it is important to establish the common ground from which everyone involved can move forward. • Look to establish shared outcomes that reflect a range of interests, not just those which are relevant to one organisation.
Be open and honest about boundaries and agendas	• Be clear about what each collaborating organisation can and cannot do, and listen to the perspectives, needs and concerns of the wider stakeholders (those you are listening to or keeping informed – see Figure 4). • Be honest with potential collaborators about your own agenda, any bottom lines and issues, and ask them to be honest with you.
Understand each other's organisations	• Who has power and influence? What's their jargon and culture? Why would they want to be involved in this collaboration?
Plan together, before doing together	• The planning stage is vital for thrashing out hidden issues, common ground, bottom lines and showstoppers. This has to be done collectively. • You will not have a successful collaboration if all the thinking and planning has only been done by one party, with others presented with a finished idea that they are asked to sign up to.

Use resources wisely	• Everyone will have limited time and money to put into the work. Discuss up front what time commitment each organisation or set of people can make and how best to use it.
Collaborative, not consultative	• Ensure any collaborative group or process is genuinely owned by the relevant players, and remains independent of any one organisation.
Share information	• Share information equally amongst the collaborators as far as possible. Access to information and knowledge becomes a very real form of power, and attention needs to be paid to how it is provided.
Show respect and invest in relationships	• Go into the process with an attitude of respect for the other stakeholders, their knowledge and interests. • Personal relationships are critical to the success of collaboration, so take the time to get to know each other.
Be representative and inclusive	• The collaboration needs to be representative of the full range of people and interests potentially affected by its work. • Map stakeholders to check who is who, and who is doing what in relation to your desired outcomes or geographical area. • Make sure there are opportunities for new people to join the collaboration.
Be responsive	• This is more than keeping people informed, it is about having a process that is responsive to the needs of the people and organisations involved. • Pay attention to all aspects of communication, from written documents to interpersonal interactions. • Consider the other partnerships, adjacent geographical areas, sectors, levels of government or governance which need to be kept informed about your work.

Be open and transparent	• Engagement should be open and transparent to all involved and to those not directly involved. • Make sure that all interested parties can clearly understand as much as possible about what is being done and why.
Reflect and learn	• This is more than exchanging information. It is about being open to making changes and adapting as new information and insights arise. • A learning, evaluative approach is needed throughout the process.

Adapted from InterAct Networks and the Environment Agency (2013).

Great meetings for great collaboration

Things will start out with informal one-to-one or small meetings or phone calls. Sooner or later, you will need to have a more weighty meeting where a bigger number of people get together to thrash out the hows and the whats.

These meetings need to be creative. You will not get the work done that you need to do, if they follow a traditional chaired format with everyone sitting around a large table and very little conversation. Neither will you get the work done if you all just turn up and see what happens. What you need is a well-planned, well-prepared participative meeting. You may want to bring in an independent facilitator to help you plan and run it. You'll want a comfortable-sized room with furniture you can move around. You'll want good clear walls that you can work on (be it whiteboards, flip charts or sticky walls). You'll need those sticky notes and chisel-tipped marker pens. This isn't a facilitation guide, so I'll stop there!

Here's what some people have said about facilitated meetings and their collaborations.

We are strongly supportive of using facilitators and teaching ourselves to use facilitation skills. It helps to have an independent facilitator so you can play your technical role. Facilitation is especially useful for the more creative meetings and larger meetings. We would not expect to use it for the business meetings where we are steering the work of the project officer. FIONA BOWLES, WESSEX WATER, TALKING ABOUT COLLABORATIVE WORK IN THE FROME AND PIDDLE CATCHMENT, UK

You need a safe space and someone providing the facilitation to move the process along. You need that third party. SIGNE BRUUN JENSEN, MAERSK LINE

There is a list of organisations I've come across who help with this kind of role at the end of the book.

> Almost everyone will be tempted to skip agreeing how to collaborate – it doesn't feel like it is taking you forward and it can be a painful conversation. But investing time in these foundations pays huge dividends.

CHAPTER 4

Finding the Common Ground – Revisiting the What

SOMETIMES THE COMMON GROUND will be obvious. Sometimes it will be easy to agree at a vague and visionary level, but less clear at a grainier level. And sometimes even the vague vision will be hard won.

The good news is that the people you begin working with are having this conversation because they want to find common ground. After all, if they can't see some potential collaborative advantage, they wouldn't have returned your phone calls.

So how can you move forward through the marshy pools of disagreement, cross-purposes and misunderstanding which inevitably litter your path?

Between meetings

In between meetings, you will rely on well-prepared documents, drafts and tracked changes, one-to-one conversations, email threads and everything else to keep the process going.

The Corporate Leaders Group on climate change is coordinated by the Cambridge Programme for Sustainability Leadership. Craig Bennett describes how he went about helping the Corporate Leaders Group put together its open letters to politicians, which are agreed by the CEOs and

Chairs who are members of that group:

The Corporate Leaders Group is made up of very senior people. Rather than get them together in big plenaries, I interviewed their 'sherpas' and formulated proposals based on hearing everyone's views. I wrote a 'pub language' version of the letter, with very simple messages and that helped us all agree what we wanted to say. In essence, this became the brief for the draft letter. Then I wrote a first proper draft. I knew which bits would be harder for some people to agree to, and I had one-to-one conversations with the two or three people who needed them. The CLG had already made it clear that they wanted me to not just be a neutral facilitator, but to challenge them to be ambitious. Then they trusted me to go away and produce a final draft. This was sent around to all the CLG members and they signed it off. We had to be very clear about timing and deadlines in advance.

Some tools for participative meetings

Even when everyone wants to find common ground, it is not easy! There was a lengthy series of steps to agree common goals and vision in the Sustainable Shipping Initiative. Signe Bruun Jensen:

This was massively difficult! We had banks, insurance brokers and shippers in the room with very different interests. Finding common interests and priorities was hard. Our four work streams for priority action emerged from an initial list of about 20. We had heated debates during several whole-day meetings. It was so important that we all had professional respect and good working relationships so that the disagreements could be worked through.

So when you do all get together, it's good to know that there are some tried and tested tools which help groups navigate this tricky territory, and you can use these in participative workshops and as ways of structuring conversations.

As noted already, this isn't a guide to facilitation skills or techniques. But there are three great tools that seem to be particularly helpful in finding common ground, so I'll take a little diversion to describe them. There are some other sources for tools at the end of the book.

Finding focal points within diversity – the post-it cluster

This tool is great for situations where there are quite a few people whose perspectives need to be shared and accommodated, and you are starting with a blank page. It takes brainstorming a step further, enabling ideas to be grouped and structured. Writing the ideas onto post-its gives you the advantages of brainstorming (many and diverse ideas generated in a small space of time) without the main disadvantages (quieter people being shouted down and 'what gets said first influences everything else').

You need a good clear wall (whiteboard, sticky wall or multiple pieces of flip chart paper), lots of large sticky notes (or A5 pieces of paper plus blu-tack or masking tape) and marker pens (to encourage writing that can be read from a few feet away).

In the context of collaboration, I'd strongly suggest that you have a bit of a conversation before beginning the brainstorming exercise, where you explain what is meant by a real-world outcome, and encourage people to write down outcomes, rather than detailed actions or vague visions.

The steps:

1. **Decide a focus question.**

   Decide a 'focus question'. It must be an open question. You need to decide how open to make it. For example, 'what outcomes do we want to achieve by working together on reducing carbon emissions' is less open than 'what outcomes do we want to achieve by working together'.

2. **Write the question up where everyone can see it.**

3. **Give out large post-it notes or other individual pieces of paper, and suitable pens.**

   The pens should be big enough to produce writing that can be read at a distance. Biros and pencils will not do.

4. **Tell people what you'd like them to do.**

   It helps to have this written up. You might want to give guidance about how many responses you'd like from each person, and how long they have got.

   You should remind people to:

   - Use one post-it per outcome – don't try to fit multiple outcomes into one sentence.
   - Write in whole sentences.
   - Write big – Not like this

5. **Give them time to write their outcomes onto post-its or paper.**

   While they are doing this, make sure your wall is set up, for example post up two or three sheets of flip chart paper, to receive the post-it notes.

6. **Bring the ideas up to the front, and cluster them.**

There are many ways of doing this ranging from a group free-for-all (where all the notes are stuck up and people move them around until some order emerges) to a very controlled process where the facilitator asks for the notes one at a time and gets everyone to agree where each one should go.

In practice, it's often a complex emergent process where the facilitator starts it off, steps back and then steps in again if needed. It's useful to ask whether there are any outcomes which are identical or very closely related to the one you are looking at. If there's disagreement about where the post-it should go, then the person who wrote it should be asked to say where they think it should go.

Expect that the clusters will need to be divided or merged as the process unfolds, and people see the range of outcomes which have been identified.

If appropriate, the clusters may be moved to be in relationship to each other – chronological order, or cause and effect, or according to some other logic.

Have some extra blu-tack or masking tape handy, in case the post-its are not sticky enough, or have been written upside down.

Note that while having lots of similar ideas in a cluster means it's likely that this is an area of common interest, the results need discussing by the group rather than being seen as a decision that the group has made.

This process doesn't, by itself, enable you to identify whether people agree or disagree about the points which have been clustered together – that will need to be explored using a different tool.

7. **Name the clusters.**

This important step is about discovering and agreeing the essence of each cluster – what is it about all of those outcomes that links them together? When the name is agreed, write it on a new piece of paper and stick it by that cluster.

8. **Optional prioritisation.**

If appropriate to the discussion, the named clusters can be assigned priority by the group. The third tool (gauging support) is a way of testing the level of commitment or priority.

9. **Optional further work to refine each cluster of outcomes.**

You may end up with some clusters which are all about, for example, restoring a stretch of river to good ecological health, or ensuring girls in a particular country go to school beyond primary age. But perhaps the proposed outcomes in a cluster are all slightly different? Perhaps the quantitative targets or end dates vary. Or maybe some are worded more precisely and others more vaguely. If the group wishes, a sub-group could be chosen to go away and find a wording to bring back as a single proposed outcome for the group to work on. The can be done within the workshop, or after it.

What do we agree about? What do we have a range of views about?

The clusters may well include outcomes related to the same issue or problem, but which are very different. They may even be contradictory. Sometimes groups are nervous about discussing areas of disagreement. This might be because they don't want to upset the good relationships which are being painstakingly built up: it might be because they fear it will not be possible to find agreement and that this is a sign of failure.

Disagreement can be positively reframed as a range of views. This can help a group to explore disagreement while minimising the anxiety associated with it.

For example:

- A group might agree that a river needs to be cleaner and healthier, and have a range of views about how they would know that it is cleaner and healthier.

- A group might agree that river water should meet legal standards, and have a range of views about good ways to ensure that this happens.

- A group might agree that it should use cost-effectiveness as a criterion for prioritising among options for taking action, and have a range of views about how to assess cost-effectiveness.

- A group might agree to set up a sub-group to come up with a proposal for assessing cost-effectiveness, and have a range of views about who might be a member of the sub-group.

What's rather lovely about this reframing, is that the group can *agree* that its members hold a range of views about something. This is a neat psychological shift which nests disagreement within an umbrella of agreement – seeing it as an acceptable, inevitable and healthy part of the group's overall purpose.

A tool which can be used to help the group embrace the range of its views is a simple sorting of statements.

1. **Generate statements or possible outcomes**

   Alone or in pairs or small groups, people write statements related to the topic under discussion. Use moveable paper, either sticky notes or A5 pieces. You will need a clear focus question – for example, 'What do we think about [this topic]?' If the post-it clustering of possible outcomes has already happened, then a cluster of outcomes which have been written already can also be used.

   The whole group can work on a number of topics or clusters at the same time, with small groups starting on one and then moving on to another once the first sorting has happened.

2. **Sort the statements or outcomes**

   Have one flip-chart titled 'we agree' and one titled 'we don't (yet) agree'. Sort the statements into those two groups. If everyone agrees with the statement or the proposed outcome, it can go on 'we agree'. If just one person doesn't agree, then it needs to go on 'we don't (yet) agree'.

   If a number of small groups have been working on different topics, then encourage people to look at the various groups' sorting. Let them move the statements: if there is something on the 'we agree' flip which someone doesn't (yet) agree with, then they can move it. Things can't be moved from 'we don't (yet) agree' – at least, not yet.

3. **Discuss the statements or outcomes which are on the 'we don't (yet) agree' flip.**

   Again in small groups, take the statements which are on the flip and, one by one, discuss them. It could be that the lack of agreement is a simple misunderstanding or the need to add a caveat which can be easily agreed. If so, write a new statement that encapsulates the agreed idea more precisely, and move it to 'we agree'.

If a statement or a suggested outcome is not agreed because of a more substantial concern, then discuss together how it would need to change, to be acceptable to all. This may be by chunking up to a more general statement: for example, from 'All new office developments to have solar panels' to 'All new office developments to utilise renewable energy sources.' Or agreement may be found by moving along the chain of cause and effect, to get closer to a real-world outcome: for example, from 'All offenders to be mentored by rehabilitated ex-offenders' to 'Reduce the % of ex-offenders who are unemployed six months after leaving prison.' Write the new statement or outcome and move it to 'we agree'.

If it is not possible to find an agreed alternative statement or outcome, then agree a description of the range of views: for example, 'We have a range of views about the benefits and downsides of onshore wind, including different levels of concern about financial cost-effectiveness and the impact on local residents. Some of us do not trust the information provided by developers about noise levels. Some of us do trust this information.' Write this description down.

4. Agree how to continue to explore the differences.

This is an optional step. You may decide that you have enough interesting areas of agreement to keep you busy, and that the best way to handle the disagreements is to agree not to work on them.

However, it may be that the areas where there is disagreement are too connected to the focus of the collaboration to be parked.

If that is the case, you will need to agree how you will continue to explore the range of views. Do you need to gather in more data or evidence to help reduce factual uncertainty? If so, you will need to agree how to research this, so that the new data is accepted by everyone as credible and trustworthy. Perhaps you all need to get to know each other better, to build trust about each other's motives. There are other reflections on uncertainty and disagreement in *Working with Uncertainty* (Acland, 2011).

At the end of this exercise, you will collectively have a much better understanding of the things you all agree about, and the things about which you have a range of views.

Are you really up for this? Gauging support

In collaboration, it's not enough that people think a particular outcome is a good thing. They need to be prepared to put real time and resources into working to achieve it. This tool helps gauge the nature of the support that each outcome has. It gives a snapshot of opinion within the group, which can then be used to inform further conversation and decision-making – it isn't a binding voting process.

You can use this once you have some prospective outcomes that you want to test with the group. The outcomes might have been identified using the post-it cluster tool, or come from some other process or source.

1. **Understand the outcomes.**

   Check that the prospective outcomes are sufficiently well understood that people can form an opinion about them. This may involve going through each one and asking if any clarification is needed, or asking someone who supports it to explain why.

2. **Stick up grids.**

   The outcomes need to be written up – perhaps on flip chart paper around the room. Once people have had a chance to thoroughly discuss and understand the outcomes, you can gauge support by posting up a grid for each outcome. Examples are shown below.

3. **People mark their view on the grids.**

   People take a pen or a sticky dot, and place their mark in one of the grid boxes for each outcome, depending on what they think their organisation's current attitude towards the outcome is. If there is more than one person present from a particular organisation, they need to work together to come to a single view. If needed, encourage people to make use of the 'don't know, don't mind' option, rather than not making a mark, as this is also useful data.

   Note that people are just putting a mark, they aren't 'signing up' their organisation to do something. That might be a later step, but this tool is just about getting a snapshot of the current level of support for the proposed shared outcomes.

FIGURE 5. Grid for gauging support A.

You might end up with a series of grids which look a bit like this:

Put a dot in one of the boxes below to show your organisation's current attitude towards this outcome	**Outcome:** For example: 'In 2016, trout can be found along the length of the River Sopping', or 'In 2015, children everywhere, boys and girls alike, will complete a full course of primary schooling' *(this is a Millennium Development Goal).*
	Would want to be (or are already) actively involved in bringing this about.
	Would like to see this happen, but it's not something we'd put time and resources into bringing about.
	Don't mind whether this happens or not, don't have a view.
	Would not like to see this happen, but it's not something we'd put time and resources into opposing.
	Would want to (or are already) actively involved in opposing this.

FIGURE 5B. Grid for gauging support B.

Put a dot in one of the boxes below to show your organisation's current attitude towards this outcome	In 2018, carbon emissions from offices are 20% lower than 2012.
● ●	Would want to be (or are already) actively involved in bringing this about.
● ● ● ● ● ● ●	Would like to see this happen, but it's not something we'd put time and resources into bringing about.
● ● ● ●	Don't mind whether this happens or not, don't have a view.
	Would not like to see this happen, but it's not something we'd put time and resources into opposing.
	Would want to (or are already) actively involved in opposing this.

This outcome is generally supported, and there are two organisations interested in putting real time into making it happen. It only takes two, to collaborate!

FIGURE 5C. Grid for gauging support C.

Put a dot in one of the boxes below to show your organisation's current attitude towards this outcome	In 2050, the UK's greenhouse gas emissions will be at least 80% lower than in 1990 *(this is the UK's Government's target, set by the Climate Change Act)*.
● ● ● ● ● ● ●	Would want to be (or are already) actively involved in bringing this about.
● ● ● ● ● ●	Would like to see this happen, but it's not something we'd put time and resources into bringing about.
●	Don't mind whether this happens or not, don't have a view.
	Would not like to see this happen, but it's not something we'd put time and resources into opposing.
	Would want to (or are already) actively involved in opposing this.

This is definitely a candidate for some serious collaboration. Seven organisations want to get active, and the rest are supportive or neutral.

FIGURE 5D. Grid for gauging support D.

Put a dot in one of the boxes below to show your organisation's current attitude towards this outcome	In 2020, there will be 13GW of onshore wind electricity generating capacity in the UK.
● ● ●	Would want to be (or are already) actively involved in bringing this about.
● ● ●	Would like to see this happen, but it's not something we'd put time and resources into bringing about.
● ● ● ● ● ●	Don't mind whether this happens or not, don't have a view.
●	Would not like to see this happen, but it's not something we'd put time and resources into opposing.
●	Would want to (or are already) actively involved in opposing this.

This one needs some serious thought and more discussion. There are three potential collaborators, but one organisation doesn't want this outcome and would actively oppose it. It's worth coming back to this and understanding better what the needs and concerns are that make this a controversial outcome, and what the common ground might be.

Once the dotting process is complete, everyone should take a good look at the grids and then discuss the implications.

Go slow to go fast

The exploration and discovery of common ground will take time. It will happen through a series of conversations, workshops and draft documents, and feel as if it's going on for ages. Don't try to rush things. Be prepared for the fact that the individuals involved in the multi-party conversations will need to go back and let their constituency (the organisation or set of organisations they represent) know how things are going, why they are headed in the direction they are, and check that this crucial set of people are happy with how things are going. Investment of time and patience at this stage is critical.

> *You take two steps forward and then check back with your own organisation and go one step back. You need to plan in time for this.* SIGNE BRUUN JENSEN, MAERSK LINE

In her work collaborating to improve a water catchment, Fiona Bowles found that some kinds of stakeholders find this role particularly challenging.

> *Collaborating was more difficult for landowners, because being a very diverse group they don't have a natural representative body, but we needed to keep our steering group small so we couldn't have them all in that group. Local authorities have almost the opposite problem, because they are such big and complex organisations with lots of specialisms and it's hard for one individual to keep their organisation informed and to know enough about all the things the organisation wants to be able to represent them. We have developed task groups to take forward particular bits of work, and that has been a good way of ensuring wider representation than we can have in the steering group.*

This 'go slow to go fast' approach is important. Cynthia Hardy and her research team (Hardy et al., 2006) in their beautifully named article 'Swimming with sharks', talk about some inevitable tensions that people working in collaboration experience: one of the tensions is balancing the tendency to either 'over identify' with the collaboration or have a 'lack of identification' with it, because of feeling loyal to your own organisation's or constituency's interests. Neither is a helpful extreme! Translating and telling the story, being a communication channel between the collaboration and the constituency takes real time, and that time needs to be factored into people's work and the overall timetable.

Ends before means

At the start, it's useful to focus on the real-world outcomes people want to see, rather than on the actions they might take to bring them about (writing a joint letter), or on the interim outcomes (getting a policy agreed by the local authority).

Of course, it will be useful and necessary to agree about actions and interim outcomes in due course, but it is easier to find agreement and to focus on the *right* actions and interim outcomes, if the ultimate outcomes are clear.

Ken Caplan, of charity Building Partnerships for Development (BPD), puts it like this:

> *The overarching mission of the partnership needs to be agreed, though partners will rarely share a common vision of how to get there. Constant dialogue is critical.* CAPLAN, 2012

There is a bit of a paradox here which all the collaborators need to sit comfortably with: collaboration only happens if there's something important that you want to get out of it, but you need to be willing to reassess what you want to get out of it, in response to what the other collaborators want. You need to have an intention, but not be so attached to your own outcome that you cannot find common ground.

Approach collaboration with an open mind, but not an empty mind.

CHAPTER 5

Formalising

IN THE EARLY STAGES, BE INFORMAL. You will need to get at least some things clearly agreed between the core collaborators – as explored in Chapter 3 – but this can be relatively rough or loose.

At some point you may want to formalise things. This could be because you need to spend some money jointly (for example, to pay for secretariat or facilitation services, research, publicity or event costs) or because you want to have some clarity about who has signed up or become a member. You may now be doing such complex and serious work together that you agree that a formal partnership is needed, or that a new organisation needs to be established to own the work and the outcomes.

The kinds of formalising document that you may choose may be a Memorandum of Understanding between two or more organisations, a Partnership Agreement, Terms of Reference for a group, ground rules for how certain kinds of meeting will operate.

The degree of detail and formality is something for the collaborators to agree between themselves. Here is a bit of a checklist that you can use, to make sure the collaborators have considered various important questions:

....

Purpose, achieving results
- Is the group/partnership clear on the point of its existence? Does it have a clear shared mission, outcomes, goals?

- Are these written down? Who has seen them?

- What documents does the group own; what's the status of these documents?

- Does the group have a process plan or work plan, with a timetable and owned actions? Is this something it intends to develop?

Membership, representativeness

- Who decides who's on the group or in the partnership, and who decides who is the Chair or fulfils other roles?

- Is membership fixed or porous? What is the formal process for joining or leaving?

- Is there a transparent, written rationale for how the group is made up, and any boundaries, for example, minimum or maximum numbers?

- Does the group sit within a hierarchy: does it report to anyone, do any other groups report to it or share information with it?

Management/high-level administration

- Does the group or partnership have a fixed life, either a date by which it will end, or a task which can be completed (rather than an expectation of an ongoing indefinite life)?

- Does the group make statements or speak as a group? If so, what's the sign-off process?

- Who administers or manages the group?

- How is the group resourced (e.g. who spends time or money, making sure it is able to function effectively)?

- Is there a Chair? Is their role set out in writing anywhere?

- Who decides what happens at meetings and how?

- How frequently does the group meet? How are dates, times and locations determined?

Legal status

- Does the group have an independent legal status, meaning it can enter into agreements or contracts with other organisations, or employ staff?

- If it doesn't, and it needs to make these kinds of agreements, how will this be handled?

BASED ON: InterAct Networks and the Environment Agency (2011).

There are some other sources of guidance about this, for example, Caplan's organisation has published *The Partnership Paperchase: Structuring Partnership Agreements in Water and Sanitation in Low-Income Communities* (Evans et al., 2004). Although this focuses on water and sanitation, the advice can be generalised to other situations.

Diversity of structures

Some collaborations do go on to become stand-alone organisations in their own right, often with complex governance structures which ensure that different parts of the system are represented in decision-making. Two examples are the Marine Stewardship Council and the Forest

Stewardship Council.

Others are supported closely by third-party organisations which provide a secretariat function, sometimes combined with expertise and a soft leadership role. The Corporate Leaders Group is convened and supported by the Cambridge Programme for Sustainability Leadership, and the Sustainable Shipping Initiative has Forum for the Future playing a similar role. There is a list of other organisations which play these third party or honest broker roles at the end of the book.

Signe Bruun Jensen is enthusiastic about what Forum for the Future brought to the Sustainable Shipping Initiative:

Forum have been brilliant in facilitating and with basic project management. They have made sure that the rest of us have used our time and resources well, arranging the phone calls and meetings and doing the admin work, gently pushing it. They have taken care of the process and provided leadership.

The pilot collaborative initiatives taking forward the catchment-based approach to improving river systems in England have had a variety of structures, including some supported by staff from one or two organisations spending a lot of their time behind the scenes bringing players together, running meetings and drafting documents. Different catchments have had different host organisations, and these have included the Environment Agency, rivers trusts such as the Thames Rivers Trust, water companies like Wessex Water and partnership-based NGOs such as Thames 21 and the Thames Estuary Partnership. This is a common pattern, with part-time support being provided by project officers who work on keeping things moving but are technically employed by one organisation, although they may be answerable to, and funded by, contributions from more than one. They may be relatively junior staff, with the leadership coming from people in collaborating organisations.

Fiona Bowles from Wessex Water sees this role as crucial:

> *If you have a collaboration but not a project officer or staff member of some kind, then very little gets done. But they need to be employed or managed jointly in some way, so that they are working for the collaboration and not just one organisation, for example through a secondment.*

Formalising is a journey of a thousand miles

There is a fascinating warts-and-all personal memoir of the early days of the Forest Stewardship Council, by Timothy Synnott (2005). He describes the early exploratory phase where governance and outcomes were being knocked around, and principles and boundaries agreed by an ever wider set of people and organisations.

This extract just gives you a flavour of how long was needed to reach agreement about governance. This is what you can expect!

> *Nearly a year passed from the San Francisco meeting to the next meeting, in March 1992. Invitations were sent out in the name of the Certification Working Group, which then effectively ceased to exist.*

> *The meeting took place in Washington D.C. in March 1992. It called itself by various names, including the FSC Working Group, the FSC Charter and the FSC Founding Group. Forty-three people*

participated from ten countries (including six tropical countries). Among the documents discussed were the third draft of the FSC Charter and Statutes. . . the fourth draft of the Forest Stewardship Standards, and the first draft of an Operations Manual for a Forest Management Evaluation and Certification System.

One of the crucial decisions at this meeting was the election of responsible officials for the FSC. After considerable disagreement and debate, this group was named "The Interim Board of the FSC Founding Group". Soon after, it started calling itself, and being called, the Interim Board of the Forest Stewardship Council. . . .

The meeting agreed the need for regional consultations around the world, national certification standards consistent with the FSC list of Principles, and a general assembly when the consultations had been completed. In addition, six work groups were set up to tackle specific issues: (1) finance, (2) membership, charter and constitution, (3) principles and criteria of forest stewardship, (4) consultative process, (5) communications, (6) monitoring other initiatives. . . .

This was the first of many FSC meetings where strong differences of opinion emerged, including some that were personalized and entrenched. Disagreements that emerged during and after the meeting included the participation of people with economic or commercial interests, and the status and decision-making powers of the "Interim Board". However, an embryonic FSC emerged from this meeting with draft statutes, standards, mission statement, and a group of people that could take decisions, raise funds, and initiate actions in its name. From then on, FSC had a de facto operational existence, although it was still 30 months away from a legal existence.

A long journey through difficult terrain, taken a step at a time, towards a sunlit upland where collaborators harness the market to protect forests and the people who depend on them.

> Don't expect collaboration to be easy: if the problem you want to tackle or the outcome you want to bring about were easy, you wouldn't need collaborators to solve it. But if the outcome is important enough, it will be worth it.

CHAPTER 6
What Kinds of Things Get Done Collaboratively?

THERE ARE SOME USEFUL THINKING TOOLS and conversation starters, which will help you share assumptions and explore choices with fellow collaborators.

Here's one from Ken Caplan, who we heard from earlier. Caplan suggests that the work done in collaboration or formal partnerships can be categorised according to whether it is rules-oriented or task-oriented, and whether it favours innovation or accountability.

....

FIGURE 6. Spirit and purpose of partnerships.

Innovation

| Experimentation around outcomes | Experimentation around outputs |
| 'What happens if we...?' | 'Let's see if together we can...' |

Rules-oriented ———————————— Task-oriented

Outputs-driven

| New institutional arrangements | 'We need to deliver X. |
| 'Can we get them to...?' | To do that we must...' |

Accountability

FROM: Caplan (2012).

....

69

Caplan says:

The top half of the matrix reflects an emphasis on synergies whereas the bottom half reflects the pressures to produce. The right side places an emphasis on outputs (tangibles like water connections) and the left side on outcomes (intangibles like increased dialogue). CAPLAN, 2003

In practice, this means that some partnerships concentrate on implementing projects, others act as rule-setters and verifiers (like the FSC and the MSC), some transfer resources from funders to the under-resourced, and some are primarily ways of enabling mutual learning and innovation.

This echoes another classic four-way categorisation of partnerships, from the work of Kenneth Kernaghan, distinguished Professor of Political Science and specialist in public administration.

Consultative	The stakeholders provide advice or recommendations, usually to a public body, possibly based on consensus, but do not make decisions or take action themselves. Describes an ongoing committee or forum, rather than a one-off consultation.
Contributory	One or more partners provide resources (time, money, expertise, information) to enable others to take action. The donors are not involved in taking action or in operational decision-making.

Operational	Collaborators share the work between them, but not the decision-making, although the operational-level work is aimed at achieving common or complementary outcomes. The decision-making may rest largely with one partner, usually the major donor or public body.
Collaborative	Decision-making power is shared, and resources (money, expertise, information, time) are pooled in some way. The risks and responsibilities for taking action implied by the decisions made, are shared, and partners give up some autonomy.

TABLE ADAPTED FROM: Kernaghan (1993) and Seidle (1995).

Craig Bennett describes how the focus of the Corporate Leaders Group changed:

To start with, its focus was one joint open letter ahead of the G8 summit in 2005. The main activities were open letters and communiques. After the disappointment of Copenhagen, we decided to get more focused on practical action so sub groups were established to take forward different strands, such as a procurement compact with government.

Being clear about their outcomes helped the core team at the centre of the Sustainable Shipping Initiative make an interesting decision about who they would 'let in'. Signe Bruun Jensen:

We took a deliberate decision not to include regulators – we framed our work as leadership going beyond regulation, as we felt that this was a niche with an opportunity to really 'raise the bar' without being embroiled in on going, and at times very static, policy discussions.

So what kind of work might collaborators do together?

The useful spectrum of collaborative working helps show the easier and more challenging activities.

FIGURE 7. Spectrum of Collaborative Working.

Exchanging information	Coordination	Cooperation	Jointly conceived/ managed/ funded initiatives or projects	Joint conception of and delivery of mainstream services, at operational level	Full strategic and operational mainstreaming, embedding collaboration so it is the new 'business as usual'.
A critical starting point for any further progress.	*'Let's not duplicate each other's activities.'*	*'Doing what we each do, in a more cooperative way.'*	*'It's our project.'*	*'We have to do this specific thing together.'*	*'It's our shared issue.'* *'We all really want this.'*

SOURCE: InterAct Networks and the Environment Agency (2013).

On the left are the less demanding forms of collaboration, which have a lower level of *collaborative advantage*. As you move towards the right-hand side, the effort goes up, and so does the potential benefit. And what inspiring outcomes there are, which can be achieved if people find that collaborative advantage! Protecting and maintaining ecosystem services, dramatically reducing poverty, limiting global temperature rises, etc. If the outcome is sufficiently compelling for the collaborators, and the wickedness of the problem demands it, then collaboration is likely to move towards the right-hand side of the spectrum.

It's not that one kind of work, or kind of partnership, is better than the other: what's important to recognise is that you and your fellow collaborators need to discuss your options and agree what you want to do together, rather than assuming that your work will be of one kind and discovering later that others have a different assumption.

CHAPTER 7

Keeping Things Going

'Who will make sure it doesn't fall over?'

This was the anxious question asked at a workshop I ran, to help a group of people set up a collaborative initiative. It was a good question. Whenever more than one person is supposedly responsible for something, there's a big risk that no-one will take responsibility.

This book is about the early stages, but it's worth thinking about how you can keep up momentum, ensure shared ownership, assess progress and review how it's going.

Remember: these things are the responsibility of all the core collaborators, not just of one organisation. Indeed, if one organisation takes on these roles too enthusiastically, the other collaborators may be subtly disempowered and before long it becomes a consultative, operational or contributory partnership rather than a collaborative one!

Having said that, there will need to be a leadership role and the person – or better, people – playing that role really need to step up to their responsibilities. Jonathon Porritt describes the experience of Forum for the Future gradually loosening their leadership of the Sustainable Shipping Initiative, so that members can take it on:

> *It has to become their initiative – to begin with they looked to Forum to draft things but they gradually got the message*

that it's their initiative, their money, their deliverables and outcomes.

So it's another of those collaboration paradoxes!

Each organisation that is involved in the collaboration will have a different way of doing things. Some people may feel that their organisation is pretty good at organising and implementing complex work involving many players and can contribute great suggestions on how to do this. Other people may think their own organisation has a poor grasp of joint working and be eager to draw on the experience of others.

Here are some tools that can help.

Decision/action record

Keeping a very clear, visible running record of decisions and the actions which flow from them can really help. A favourite way of doing this is to have a flip chart sheet posted up with columns for decision, actions, lead names and deadlines.

Bring the actual flips to the next meeting, to help jog people's memories and to show that actions and decisions are meant to last to the next meeting, not fade away. Circulate a note (this could even be a photo of the flip chart paper) very soon after the meeting, so people have a record of what they've committed to.

FIGURE 8. Example decision/action record.

DECISION	ACTION	WHO	BY WHEN
Our collaboration needs suppliers to be represented.	Ask RW to provide some warm contacts.	PW	7th Nov
	Divide up contacts and each phone at least one.	PW KH LW	14th Nov
	Share results of those phone calls – who's interested?	PW KH LW	21st Nov
Work on labour standards is our priority.	Write first draft of our outcomes, based on today. Place on O Drive.	RT & KH	31st Oct
	Circulate to this group for comments.	RT	31st Oct

SOURCE: InterAct Networks and the Environment Agency (2012b).

And of course anyone who is at the meeting, and who has the right skills, authority or resources can take on an action: it doesn't have to be someone from the organisation which first brought people together.

Keeping wider constituencies engaged

It's crucial to maintain links with the wider constituencies, to stop the collaboration spiralling off and leaving them behind. Action points in meetings can routinely include checking that each collaborator is clear who they are representing or reporting to, and how they will do that. At the end of each meeting, once the decision/action record has been made, everyone present should agree a statement about the meeting that collaborators can use to report back to their constituencies. It's particularly important to agree how to talk about any sensitive issues.

Check in on progress

Don't wait for the next meeting to find out how the actions are going. Everyone who has an action can be sent a friendly email or phoned up to find out how it's going. This can help flush out problems with the actions early enough to share the problem with the group and find a way of solving it before the next meeting. Perhaps one of the actions which can be taken on is checking up on actions on behalf of the group!

One way of doing this is to organise regular very short conference calls where participants share:

- how they are feeling

- one thing they've done

- one thing they're going to do

- the help that they need.

Once people have become familiar with this agenda and know that they are only expected (or allowed) to say one thing, the calls can be very short – say, 15 minutes. Those who can't ring in can make their input by email.

Discuss how it's going

Include 'reflecting on how we're working together' as a meeting aim, and ask people whether they are satisfied with the way the group is deciding things and how well it is doing in allocating and delivering actions. What's working well? What's getting in the way? Are decisions clear enough and built on strong enough foundations? How well are decisions lasting from one meeting to the next? Does anything need to change about this?

It's not easy to raise the awkward subject of poor working practices in the normal course of things, which is why a more formal review stage with a checklist or set of questions can help. Fiona Bowles says:

> *Some people had trouble reading information before the meeting and being prepared. But we haven't really done anything to challenge this. Something we did learn, though, was the importance of understanding the different situations of people being there voluntarily and those who are being paid to be there. We agreed to pay expenses, to make it easier for those unfunded people.*

Absent friends

The group needs to agree about what to do if a particular person or organisation is not able to attend a meeting. Do they have to live with whatever the rest of the group decides? Can they send someone else in their place? What responsibility does the group have to notice when a key perspective or organisation is missing from the discussion, and take this into account in its thinking and to ensure that the absent person is briefed on what happened? What can everyone do to make sure that people know what is likely to come up so that they can input their views before the meeting?

Much of this section was based on InterAct Networks and the Environment Agency (2012a).

Review points – how and what

When significant phases of work are coming to an end it is a good idea to organise a more in-depth review which elicits feedback about the wider process – the how – and gives the people who are at the core of the collaboration, facilitating or leading it, the chance to understand the feedback and decide what to do about it.

You could seek feedback from collaborators and wider stakeholders via a survey and then present the results to the core collaborators so they can draw their own conclusions. They could ask themselves questions like:

- Did we meet our aims for this phase of work?

- Are we structured in the right way for the next phase?

- Are the right people and organisations involved?

- Are we working together effectively and efficiently?

- What needs to change about how we're doing things?

And of course, you can use the principles of collaborative working (above) as a framework for collectively reviewing how you're working together.

You'll also want to review progress towards the *what*. Beware! Collaborative working takes longer and success may look different to how you expected it to look when you first set out. So be prepared to do some quite sophisticated thinking about whether you are achieving what you want to achieve, through the collaboration.

Much of this section is based on InterAct Networks and the Environment Agency (2012b).

CHAPTER 8

Case Studies

Collaborating at catchment level in England – Frome and Piddle

IN ENGLAND, the government encouraged people and organisations to get together and see what more they can achieve for rivers and other water bodies, if they take a 'catchment' based approach. This means working with the system which is contributing to the health or otherwise of rivers, lakes, underground water and so on. Some catchments were provided with resources to pilot ways of collaborating. One of these catchments was the Frome and Piddle in Dorset (**http://www.wessexwater.co.uk/ environment/threecol.aspx?id=7525**). The collaborators included the Environment Agency, National Farmers' Union, West Dorset District Council and Wessex Water, which is the local water company and hosted the pilot.

Early work included getting a really good understanding of the current state of the system, and agreeing criteria and a methodology for prioritising among different options for taking action to tackle the various problems. There was already a history of strategies and plans and some good stakeholder engagement in the area around water issues, which gave the collaborators a head start. The area has a large farming community and the next phase of work includes engaging them more in reviewing progress.

Fiona Bowles of Wessex Water, explains why collaboration is needed in this kind of situation:

Many of the water quality issues identified arise through land management (e.g. agriculture, highways) as well as sewage discharges, so to resolve these the beneficiaries of good water quality (such as fishery owners, water companies, the harbour authorities) need to collaborate with those who can deliver the protection.

Within our own business, Wessex Water has to provide clean drinking water and to treat sewage. We prefer to reduce the pollution (nitrate and pesticides) getting in to the water in the first place, rather than spending a lot of money taking out the pollution later. So it's the farmers, not the water company, who ultimately will be taking action to protect drinking water. So collaboration is key.

Prince of Wales' Corporate Leaders Group on Climate Change

First set up to give a focus for progressive business leaders to have a voice on climate change issues, this exclusive collaboration is facilitated by the Cambridge Programme for Sustainability Leadership (CPSL) (http://www.cpsl.cam.ac.uk/Business-Platforms/The-Prince-of-Wales-Corporate-Leaders-Group-on-Climate-Change/UK-CLG.aspx). Their first joint work was an open letter to then Prime Minister Tony Blair ahead of the G8 Summit in Gleneagles in 2005. More open letters and communiques have followed, with an EU and international Corporate Leaders Groups being established too. Members are from major companies such as

Shell, BT, Sky and Unilever and are expected to be involved at CEO, Chair or other Board level. Working groups typically involve senior VPs, Group Climate Change advisers or similarly senior experts (The Prince of Wales' UK Corporate Leaders Group, 2013).

This strong stipulation about only including senior figures is part of what gives the Corporate Leaders Group its credibility and weight. Having begun with a focus on influencing government policy at national, regional and international level, the Corporate Leaders Group is also now developing projects to demonstrate the potential of low carbon solutions, for example, exploring the use of procurement as a way of driving innovation.

Craig Bennett, who worked for CPSL supporting the Corporate Leaders Group, explains what the CLG wanted:

> *CPSL had a very clear brief from key members: they didn't want to be just another business lobby group with lowest common denominator ambition and positions. They wanted to find their highest common denominator, and our role as CPSL was partly to hold them to that ambition.*

Sustainable Shipping Initiative

Working at an international level, this is also primarily a business collaboration, working across the entire value chain of the shipping industry. But rather than focusing on influencing government policy, the Sustainable Shipping Initiative wants to test out ways of solving some of the system-level barriers to using more fuel-efficient technologies in the global shipping sector. There are some classic split incentives and complex relationships between ship builders, owners, those companies that charter boats and their clients which, according to Jonathon Porritt, mean that 'there are limitless opportunities to pass the buck and real disadvantages to first movers'. So synchronised movement coordinated by the businesses that want to be leaders is essential.

The Sustainable Shipping Initiative is managed by Forum for the Future with input from WWF, and its key members include Maersk Line, Unilever, Cargill, ABN AMRO and Lloyd's Register (**http://ssi2040.org/**). It is on its way to being formalised as a stand-alone body with a membership structure and voting rules being developed. Forum for the Future has used a clear four-stage approach to organise the work of the Sustainable Shipping Initiative: starting with a 'case for action' baseline, moving on to developing a shared vision, followed by practical work streams. This third stage includes how to finance sustainable shipping to overcome the split incentives, and technological innovation. The fourth stage will be about spreading those innovations beyond the Sustainable Shipping Initiative's members to the wider shipping sector.

Marine Stewardship Council

The longest-running of our collaboration examples, the Marine Stewardship Council was modelled on the Forest Stewardship Council. Its focus is the development of a science-based standard for sustainable fisheries which is used by independent auditors to certify fisheries. The fisheries standard is supported by a traceability standard that ensures that only fish coming from certified sustainable fisheries ends up on sale with the MSC label. Together these standards enable food companies, retailers, restaurants and consumers to confidently make more ethical seafood purchasing decisions (http://www.msc.org/). MSC puts it like this: 'Our vision is of the world's oceans teeming with life, and seafood supplies safeguarded for this and future generations' (Marine Stewardship Council, undated). By April 2013, 200 fisheries had been certified as sustainable. This represents about 8% of the annual global harvest of wild caught fish and means that there are around 19,500 different seafood products on sale worldwide that display the MSC's distinctive blue-fish-tick label.

The MSC has detailed institutional rules which include having certain numbers of seats on its main Board of Trustees set aside for each of three sectors (Seafood, Conservation and Market). Institutional rules also establish a separate Stakeholder Council with co-chairs from a Public Interest Chamber and a Commercial Chamber each holding a seat on the main board; and a Technical Advisory Board made up of scientific and technical experts, the chair of which also sits on the main board.

....

CHAPTER 9

Summary of First Steps

SO THE REALISATION CREEPS UP ON YOU, or you have a light-bulb moment: to get what I want, systemic change is needed and it can only come about through collaborating. Or someone else has this realisation, and invites you to come and play.

You sound people out, inside and outside your organisation. Does this idea seem like a runner? You're into the early exploratory phase.

Good news! At least one other person or organisation agrees that they have a common or complementary outcome that they want to achieve, and you think you can usefully work together to take it forward.

So now you begin to grow that core group of early collaborators, and plot together the what, the who and the how.

And you plan and do, plan and do, learning more about how to work well together as it goes along.

And you review – the what, the who and the how.

And you plan and do, plan and do some more.

And depending on how things go and what's needed, a new stand-alone organisation or group with a life of its own may spin off, or you may decide you've achieved as much together as you want or can, and the collaboration comes to a natural end.

I asked Signe Bruun Jensen of Maersk for her advice:

The early stages are heavily dependent on personalities. Keep an open mind. Be willing to see where it goes, jump in and see where it takes you!

....

References

Acland, A., 2011. *Working with Uncertainty*. Available at: **http://bit.ly/ 12dJ6f3** [accessed 16 April 2013].

Acland, A., undated. Dialogue Top 10 – Principles and Characteristics of Stakeholder Dialogue. *Elements*, pp. 25–27. Available at: **http://bit.ly/ 14b9R6n** [accessed 20 June 2013].

Ansell, C. and Gash, A., 2007. Collaborative governance in theory and practice. *Journal of Public Administration Research and Theory* (Volume 18): 543–571.

Caplan, K., 2003. *Plotting Partnerships: Ensuring Accountability and Fostering Innovation*. Available at: **http://bit.ly/10E1bIR** [accessed 18 April 2013].

Caplan, K., 2012. *Partnerships in Practice: Getting Away from the Rhetoric* (Cambridge: Cambridge Programme for Sustainability Leadership).

Evans, B., McMahon, J. and Caplan, K., 2004. *The Partnership Paperchase: Structuring Partnership Agreements in Water and Sanitation in Low-Income Countries* (London: BDP Water and Sanitation).

Frank, F., Smith, A. and Canada Human Resources Development Canada, 2000. *The Partnership Handbook* (Toronto: Minister of Public Works and Government Services Canada).

Hardin, G., 1968. The tragedy of the commons. *Science* (Vol. 162, No. 3859): 1243–1248.

Hardy, C., Lawrence, T.B. and Phillips, N., 2006. Swimming with sharks: Creating strategic change through multi-sector collaboration. *International Journal of Strategic Change Management* (Vol. 1, Nos 1/2): 96–112.

Huxham, C., 1993. Pursuing collaborative advantage. *The Journal of the Operational Research Society* (Vol. 44, No. 6): 599–611.

InterAct Networks and the Environment Agency, 2011. *Principles and Practice for Collaborative Working – Training for Catchment Pilots, Training Manual* (Bristol: The Environment Agency).

InterAct Networks and the Environment Agency, 2012a. Pilot Catchments Collaborative Working Learning Bulletin #1.

InterAct Networks and the Environment Agency, 2012b. Pilot Catchments Collaborative working Learning Bulletin #2.

InterAct Networks and the Environment Agency, 2013. *Introduction to Collaborative Working, Training Manual* (Bristol: The Environment Agency).

Kernaghan, K., 1993. Partnership and public administration: Conceptual and practical considerations. *Canadian Public Administration* (Vol. 36, No. 1): 57–76.

Marine Stewardship Council, undated. *Vision and Mission*. Available at: http://www.msc.org/about-us/vision-mission [accessed 19 April 2013].

Rittel, H.W.J. and Webber, M.M., 1973. Dilemmas in a general theory of planning (http://www.uctc.net/mwebber/Rittel+Webber+Dilemmas+General_Theory_of_Planning.pdf). *Policy Sciences* (Vol. 4): 155–169.

Seidle, L.F., 1995. *Rethinking the Delivery of Public Services to Citizens* (Montreal: Institute for Research on Public Policy).

Sustainable Shipping Initiative, 2012. *SSI Financing Sustainable Shipping* (London: Sustainable Shipping Initiative).

Synnott, T., 2005. *Some notes on the early years of the FSC.* Available at: https://ic.fsc.org/our-history.17.htm [accessed 9 April 2013].

The Prince of Wales' UK Corporate Leaders Group, 2013. *Membership Brochure* (Cambridge: Cambridge Programme for Sustainability Leadership).

Further Reading on Tools to Use in Meetings

Chambers, R., 2002. *Participatory workshops: A Sourcebook of 21 Sets of Ideas and Activities* (London: Earthscan).

Holman, P., Devane, T., and Cady, S. (eds), 2007. *The Change Handbook: The Definitive Resource on Today's Best Methods for Engaging Whole Systems* (San Francisco, CA: Berrett-Koehler).

Useful Organisations

IN THEIR OWN WORDS...

Ag Innovations Network:
http://aginnovations.org/

Ag Innovations Network brings people together to build a food system that works for all. Ag Innovations Networks are facilitators of crucial conversations, conveners of meetings that matter, and enablers of change.

Building Partnerships for Development (BPD):
http://www.bpd-waterandsanitation.org/

A non-profit charity that improves the provision of water and sanitation services in unserved and poorly served communities by ensuring that partnerships are effective and appropriately ambitious.

Cambridge Programme for Sustainability Leadership (CPSL):
http://www.cpsl.cam.ac.uk/

Founded in 1988, the University of Cambridge Programme for Sustainability Leadership (CPSL) is an institution within the School of Technology of the University of Cambridge and is dedicated to working with leaders from business, government and civil society on the critical global challenges of the 21st century.

Forum for the Future:
http://www.forumforthefuture.org/

A sustainability non-profit working globally with business, government and others to solve tricky challenges.

InterAct Networks:
http://www.interactnetworks.co.uk/

Helps organisations that want to talk, listen and collaborate better with stakeholders and the public. InterAct Networks improves people's engagement skills and works with them to embed engagement in their day-to-day work.

Natural Innovation:
http://www.natural-innovation.net/links/

Part of the Hara Collaborative, Natural Innovation is an interdisciplinary platform for learning and collaboration around the pressing issues of our time and the new human capacities needed to tackle them. Our work focuses on participatory process design and facilitation and initiating collaborative social innovation projects.

Partnership Brokers Association:
http://partnershipbrokers.org/

The Partnership Brokers Association's vision is to create a more equitable and sustainable world by building capacity for innovation, efficiency and excellence in cross-sector collaboration.

Reos Partners:
http://reospartners.com/

A social innovation consultancy that addresses complex, high-stakes challenges around the world. We help teams of stakeholders work together on their toughest challenges.

The Environment Council:
http://www.the-environment-council.org.uk/

The Environment Council's mission is to develop and promote good ways of engaging people in discussions and decisions to make sustainable development happen. Our vision is a world where people are actively engaged in decisions to make sustainable development the way we all live.

The Partnering Initiative:
http://thepartneringinitiative.org/

The Partnering Initiative works with individuals, organisations, partnerships and systems to inspire, promote and support the use of cross-sector partnerships worldwide.

....

For Product Safety Concerns and Information please contact our EU
representative GPSR@taylorandfrancis.com
Taylor & Francis Verlag GmbH, Kaufingerstraße 24, 80331 München, Germany